NATIONAL GEOGRAPHIC KiDS

DOGGY DEFENDERS

DOLLEY

★ ★ ★

THE FIRE DOG

Lisa M. Gerry
Photographs by Lori Epstein

NATIONAL GEOGRAPHIC
WASHINGTON, D.C.

★ ★ ★

Meet DOLLEY!

★ ★ ★

Dolley is a Labrador retriever.

Like most dogs,
she loves getting snuggles ...

... and playing fetch!

But Dolley is also different from other dogs. She has a job!

Dolley is a **fire dog.**

Dolley's partner is her owner,

Captain Herndon.

Each day, they go to the **fire station.**

There is a lot
of work for the
firefighters—and
for Dolley, too!

Dolley's job is very important. When there is a fire, she sniffs out what started it.

Dolley can smell a drop of fire-starting liquid

that is smaller than a coin.

Dolley works hard to keep her **super sniffer** in tip-top shape. Captain Herndon helps Dolley practice by hiding scents for her to find.

Is it hidden in this can? Yes! Dolley gets a **tasty reward** for finding the scent.

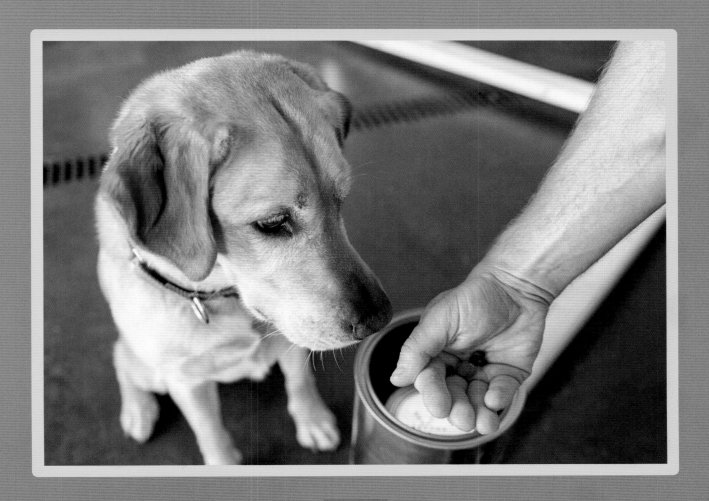

Sometimes Captain Herndon hides the scent outside, at a special place called a burn house. Then he says to Dolley, "Seek!"

Dolley's off!

She sniffs all around to find
what Captain Herndon hid.

Sniff, sniff!

Dolley uses her **strong nose** to search up high ... and down low.

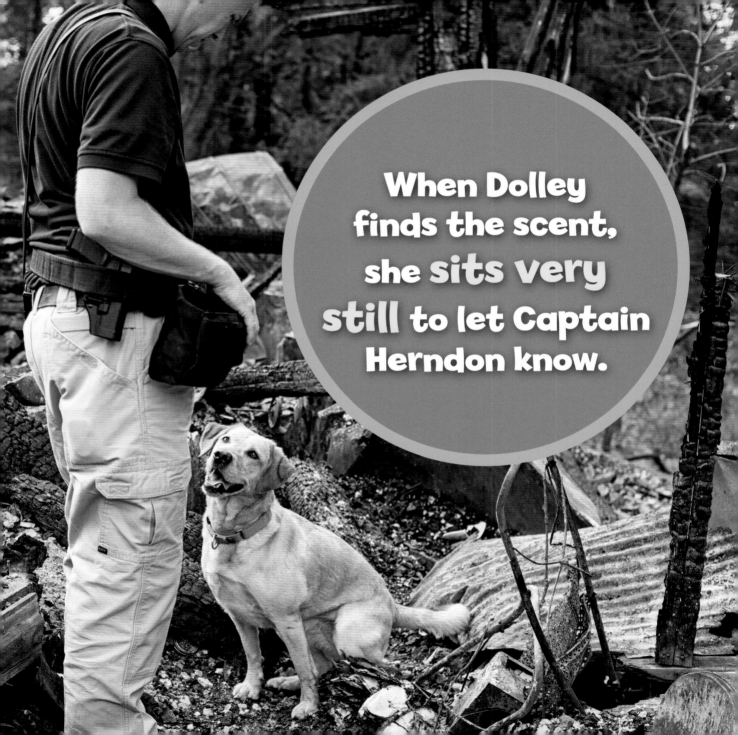

When Dolley finds the scent, she sits very still to let Captain Herndon know.

Good job, Dolley!

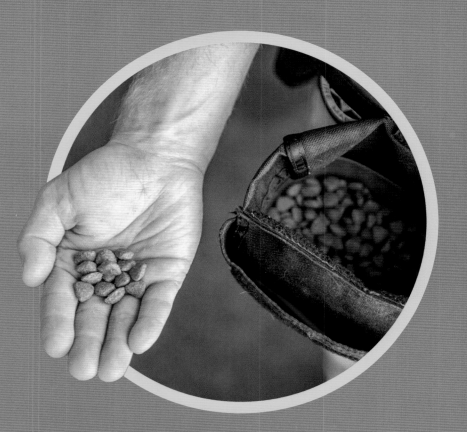

And now for the yummy part—Dolley gets some kibble as a reward. Mmm!

After a fun time practicing, Dolley gets **cleaned up.** Captain Herndon uses a special tool to wash her paws.

One, two, three, four ... all done!

Next, Dolley helps kids practice fire safety!

Dolley shows kids how to prevent fires and stay safe if there is a fire.

She also teaches them to stop, drop, and roll!

Now it's time for Dolley to stop practicing.

Captain Herndon has gotten a call—there is a **real fire!**

When Dolley and Captain Herndon arrive, the other firefighters have put out the flames. It's Dolley's turn to do her job!

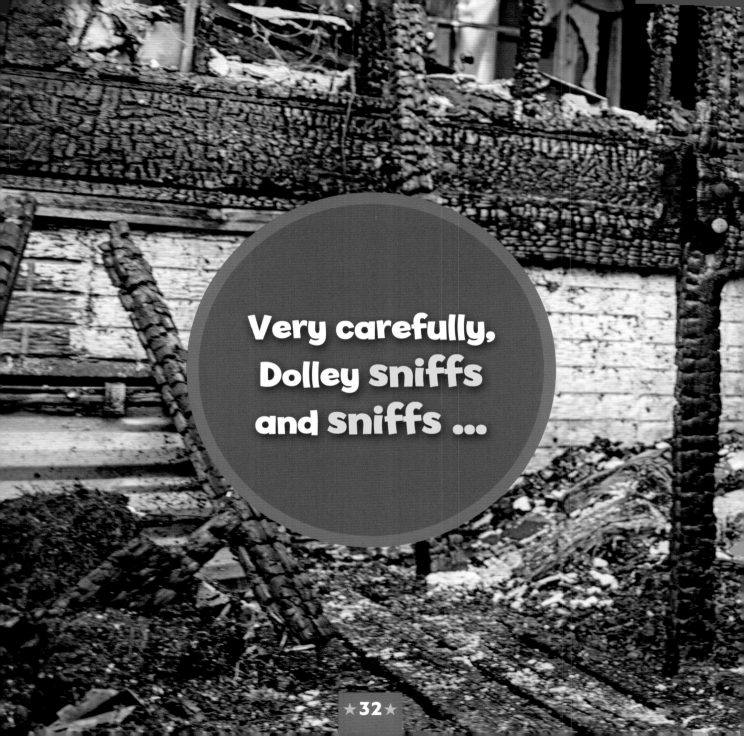

Very carefully, Dolley sniffs and sniffs ...

... and **sniffs** and **sniffs.**

Suddenly, she sits down. Dolley has found the cause of the fire! Now the firefighters know where it started. Good job, Dolley!

But all that hard work has made Dolley dirty.

Oh no! Another bath?

Dolley shake, shake, shakes to get dry, and then gets wrapped in a warm, cozy towel.

It's been a long day, and Dolley is ready to go home with Captain Herndon. Now she can **relax** with her family ...

... and play!

Dolley loves her job, but she also loves being an off-duty dog.

At work or at home,
Dolley is always a hero.
Good job, Dolley!

Sweet dreams!

Meet the Team!

Captain Herndon answers questions about Dolley and being a fire investigator.

Q How did you get Dolley?

A I was paired with Dolley through the ATF, the Bureau of Alcohol, Tobacco, Firearms and Explosives. The ATF is a law enforcement agency in the United States' Department of Justice.

Q Who trained Dolley?

A The ATF trained Dolley for 12 weeks.

Squirt

Jimmy

Dolley

Q **What do you and Dolley do in your free time?**

A Dolley likes to play fetch or relax, though she's usually very busy!

Q **What is Dolley's favorite game?**

A She loves to swim.

Q **What is the best part of being a fire investigator?**

A The best part of being a fire investigator for the Loudoun County Fire Marshal's Office is getting to help people who are in need, especially during emergencies.

Dolley's Safety Tips

Dolley is an expert at fire safety—and you can be, too! Follow these tips to help prevent fires, and to know what to do in case of an emergency.

1. **Never play with fire, and report those that do to local authorities.**

2. **Know how to dial 9-1-1 and be able to provide your address.**

3. **Have a smoke alarm on every floor of your home and one in every bedroom.**

4. **Change the batteries in your smoke alarms every six months (you can do this when you change your clocks in the spring and fall).**

5. **Replace your smoke alarms every 10 years.**

6. Have an exit plan for emergencies. The plan should include two ways to get outside and a meeting spot. Remember to practice your exit plan often.

7. Consider closing your bedroom door at night to prevent smoke and heat from entering your room if there is an emergency.

8. In case of a fire, check all doors for heat before opening them.

9. During an emergency, never hide—go outside. Once you are outside, stay outside.

10. If your clothes catch fire, remember to stop, drop, and roll.

LOUDOUN COUNTY

Since 1888, the National Geographic Society has funded more than 12,000 research, exploration, and preservation projects around the world. The Society receives funds from National Geographic Partners, LLC, funded in part by your purchase. A portion of the proceeds from this book supports this vital work. To learn more, visit natgeo.com/info.

NATIONAL GEOGRAPHIC and Yellow Border Design are trademarks of the National Geographic Society, used under license.

For more information, visit nationalgeographic.com, call 1-800-647-5463, or write to the following address:

National Geographic Partners
1145 17th Street N.W.
Washington, D.C. 20036-4688 U.S.A.

Visit us online at nationalgeographic.com/books
For librarians and teachers: ngchildrensbooks.org
More for kids from National Geographic:
natgeokids.com

National Geographic Kids magazine inspires children to explore their world with fun yet educational articles on animals, science, nature, and more. Using fresh story-telling and amazing photography, Nat Geo Kids shows kids ages 6 to 14 the fascinating truth about the world—and why they should care.
kids.nationalgeographic.com/subscribe

For information about special discounts for bulk pur-chases, please contact National Geographic Books Special Sales: specialsales@natgeo.com

For rights or permissions inquiries, please contact National Geographic Books Subsidiary Rights:
bookrights@natgeo.com

Designed by Callie Broaddus

The publisher would like to thank Lisa Gerry, author; Lori Epstein, photographer; Paige Towler, project editor; Shannon Hibberd, photo editor; and Dolley, Captain Herndon, Dolley's family, the entire Loudoun County Combined Fire and Rescue System, and Briggs Animal Adoption Center for their support and dedication to their communities.

Hardcover ISBN: 978-1-4263-3299-9
Reinforced library binding ISBN: 978-1-4263-3300-2

Printed in China
19/PPS/1

W9-CKI-167

the BAD GUYS

in

ALIEN VS
BAD GUYS

TEXT AND ILLUSTRATIONS COPYRIGHT © 2017 BY AARON BLABEY

ALL RIGHTS RESERVED. PUBLISHED BY SCHOLASTIC INC., PUBLISHERS SINCE 1920, 557 BROADWAY,
NEW YORK, NY 10012. SCHOLASTIC AND ASSOCIATED LOGOS ARE TRADEMARKS AND/OR REGISTERED TRADEMARKS
OF SCHOLASTIC INC. THIS EDITION PUBLISHED UNDER LICENSE FROM SCHOLASTIC AUSTRALIA PTY LIMITED.
FIRST PUBLISHED BY SCHOLASTIC AUSTRALIA PTY LIMITED IN 2017.

THE PUBLISHER DOES NOT HAVE ANY CONTROL OVER AND DOES NOT ASSUME ANY
RESPONSIBILITY FOR AUTHOR OR THIRD-PARTY WEBSITES OR THEIR CONTENT.

NO PART OF THIS PUBLICATION MAY BE REPRODUCED, STORED IN A RETRIEVAL SYSTEM, OR TRANSMITTED IN ANY
FORM OR BY ANY MEANS, ELECTRONIC, MECHANICAL, PHOTOCOPYING, RECORDING, OR OTHERWISE, WITHOUT WRITTEN
PERMISSION OF THE PUBLISHER. FOR INFORMATION REGARDING PERMISSION, WRITE TO SCHOLASTIC AUSTRALIA, AN
IMPRINT OF SCHOLASTIC AUSTRALIA PTY LIMITED, 345 PACIFIC HIGHWAY, LINDFIELD NSW 2070 AUSTRALIA.

THIS BOOK IS A WORK OF FICTION. NAMES, CHARACTERS, PLACES, AND INCIDENTS ARE EITHER THE PRODUCT OF
THE AUTHOR'S IMAGINATION OR ARE USED FICTITIOUSLY, AND ANY RESEMBLANCE TO ACTUAL PERSONS,
LIVING OR DEAD, BUSINESS ESTABLISHMENTS, EVENTS, OR LOCALES IS ENTIRELY COINCIDENTAL.

ISBN 978-1-338-18959-9

10 9 8 7 6 5 4 3   18 19 20 21 22

PRINTED IN THE U.S.A.   23
FIRST U.S. PRINTING 2018

AARON BLABEY
the BAD GUYS
in
ALIEN vs BAD GUYS
SCHOLASTIC INC.

GOOD GUYS CLUB SAVES THE WORLD!

There are celebrations across the globe tonight, as the evil

DR. RUPERT MARMALADE

has been **DEFEATED!**

TIFFANY FLUFFIT

6 NEWS

Yes, that's right—every kitten, puppy, bunny, pony, and dolphin has been turned from a **FLESH-EATING ZOMBIE BACK** into our cute and furry friends! And **WHO** do we have to thank?

THE GOOD GUYS CLUB!

AS GOOD AS IT GETS!

Sure, the name might be lame, but I doubt there's a creature on this planet that wouldn't like to give those **WONDERFUL, WHOLESOME BOYS** a hug!

The **LOVABLE**
Mr. Wolf!

The **BRILLIANT**
Mr. Snake!

The **POWERFUL**
Mr. Shark!

And
THE OTHER ONE
that is some kind of fish.
Possibly a sardine.

They are the **GREATEST LEGENDS OF OUR TIME!**

ARTIST'S RENDERING

And I'd personally like to add that I **ALWAYS** thought they were awesome.

I really did . . .

So let's send them all a great, big . . .

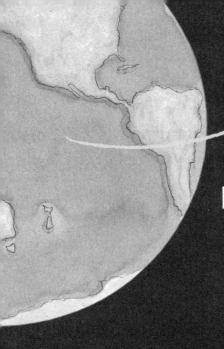

THANK-YOU,
wherever they may be!

To the gang that saved
the world—
NOT BAD, GUYS . . .
not bad at all!

It's nice to think of you out there . . .

wherever you are . . .

protecting us . . .

you GREAT, BIG, BEAUTIFUL TOUGH GUYS . . .

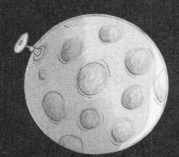

· CHAPTER 1 ·
DEEP SPACE, DEEP POOP

I think I'm
going to cry . . .

Me too . . .

Pull yourselves together, will you?

WE HAVE TO GET OUT OF HERE!

How?! **HE'S AN ALIEN!** Marmalade **ISN'T** a guinea pig. Or even the mad scientist who tried to destroy the world. He's an enormous hostile alien life-form with **MORE TEETH, TENTACLES,** and **BUTTS** than any decent creature should have . . .

And we're trapped inside its space station on the moon **WITHOUT A ROCKET.**

So **HOW ARE WE GOING TO GET OUT OF HERE?!**

Shhh! It'll hear us! What are we going to do? We can't hide here forever . . .

Oh man, this is SO not fair.
We've come so far!
Finally, everyone thinks we're
heroes! We can't die here.
We need a plan . . .

Hey! What's *that*?

Legs!
*Where are
you going?!*

SCUTTLE!

SCUTTLE!

SCUTTLE!

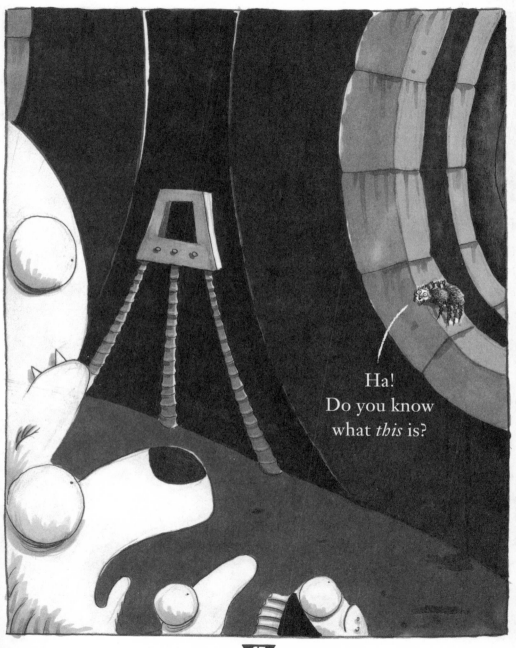

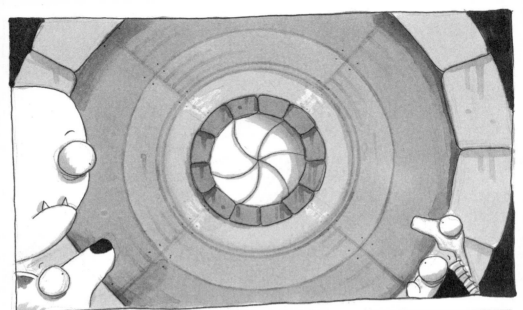

Is it the little room where we all die?

But this is an
ALIEN SPACESHIP!
How will you even know how to work it?

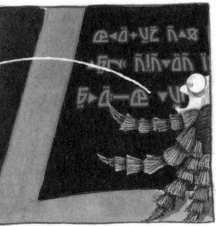

How hard can it be? I bet there are a whole **BUNCH OF LANGUAGES** on here and probably some from **EARTH** and . . . yep . . . what if I just punch in a few **COORDINATES** and . . . yep . . .

ready to launch

destination > earth

I'd say we're good to go!

Man, you just **HACKED AN ALIEN COMPUTER!** Seriously, we don't give you as much credit as you deserve. Let's hear it for Legs, guys!

OK, I'll tell you what— why don't you stay here and **HAVE A PARADE FOR LEGS,** and I'll see you back on Earth. OK?

You are the rudest little—

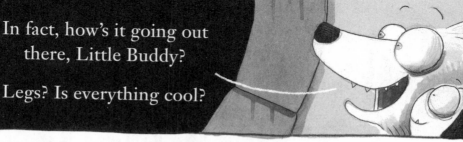

· CHAPTER 2 ·
AND THEN THERE WERE FOUR

LEGS?!

Oh no, this isn't
good at all . . .

Where is he?!

Hey, you
know what?

The ole escape pod is all
GOOD TO GO,
so I say we just jump right
back in and skedaddle,
whaddya say?

Are you serious?

YEAH!
I mean, there are **PLENTY** of these pod things. Legs can just take the **NEXT ONE**. He's probably just gone to **GRAB A SANDWICH** or something, and I'm sure he wouldn't mind if we took off and met him back on—

NO ONE LEAVES UNTIL WE FIND LEGS. GOT IT?

I mean, yeah, we **COULD** do that, but don't you think it makes more sense to—

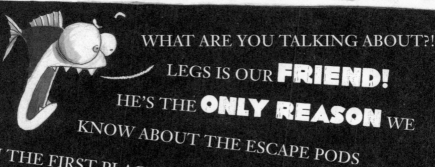

WHAT ARE YOU TALKING ABOUT?!

LEGS IS OUR **FRIEND!**

HE'S THE **ONLY REASON** WE KNOW ABOUT THE ESCAPE PODS IN THE FIRST PLACE, AND **YOU WANT TO LEAVE HIM BEHIND?!**

Hey, Piranha! Keep it down!

NO! I'VE HAD IT UP TO HERE WITH THIS ROTTEN LITTLE *DIABLO!*

I'm just **SAYING**, I think Legs would **WANT** us to save—

YOU ARE THE MOST SELFISH . . .

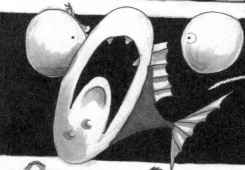

Piranha!

MEAN-HEARTED . . .

Really, man—*shush!*

SON OF A WORM I'VE EVER . . .

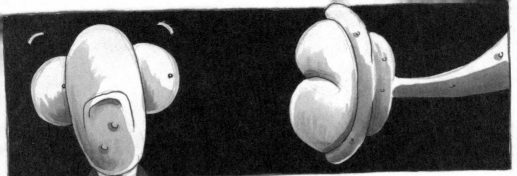

Is it just me, or do I have an **ALIEN BUTT** pointed at my face?

Piranha! *Look out!*

SPLODGE!
SPLODGE!
Oh my stars!
It uses its
BUTTS AS HANDS!
NO!
TOO
MANY . . .

PIRANHA!

That's it. I'm out of here.

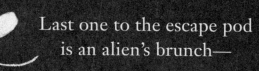

Last one to the escape pod is an alien's brunch—

Don't even think about it. We have to go after him.

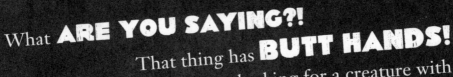

What **ARE YOU SAYING?!**
That thing has **BUTT HANDS!**
You really want to go looking for a creature with
great, big, **POOPY**
BUTT
HANDS?!

Shut up and listen!

TOOOOOOOOO MAANNNYYYYYY

BUUUUUTTTTTSSSSSSSSSSS!!!

He's still ALIVE!
We can follow his voice!

Let's go!

But what about the escape pod?
Maybe I should stay here and
look after it, just in case . . .

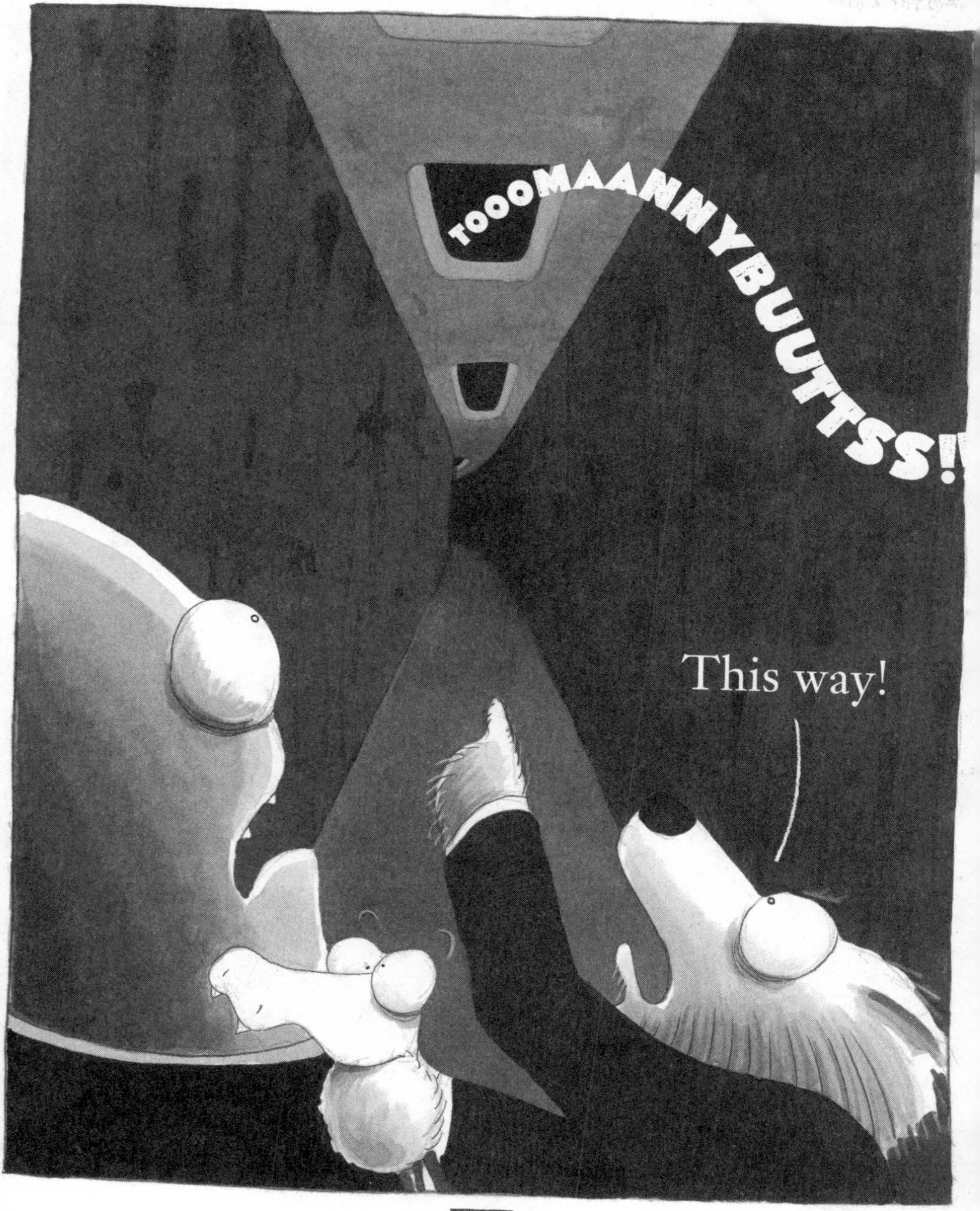
TOOOMAAANNYBUUTTSS!!
This way!

· CHAPTER 3 ·
THE LADY ALIEN

OK, if you vote to stop looking for our friends, raise your hands.

No hands? OK, then, **LET'S KEEP LOOKING!**

Oh, you're hilarious.
I hope the alien takes
you next.

You should be
so lucky—

AAAAARRRGH!
IT'S GOT
ME!

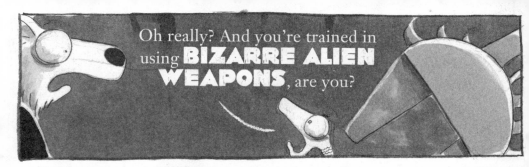

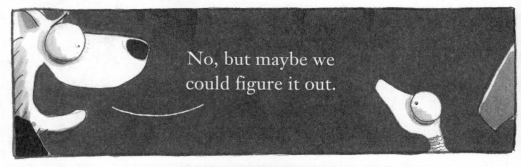

SHARK?!
Man, you are SO
good at disguises.

I know.

But how did you manage
to make this so quickly?

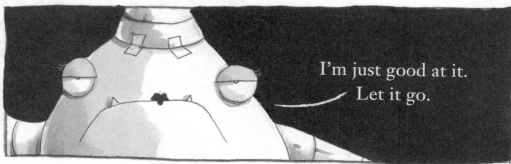

I'm just good at it.
Let it go.

What's with the **DRESS?!**

I'm going to pretend to be a **LADY ALIEN**. And when the **MARMALADE ALIEN** tries to make friends with me, I'll get him to show us where he keeps the creatures that he's captured and **BINGO**— we can rescue the guys. **THAT'S** the plan.

OK, your disguises may have worked in the past, but what you just said is so stupid it makes me want to eat my own face.

Well, I like it.

IT'S INSANE!

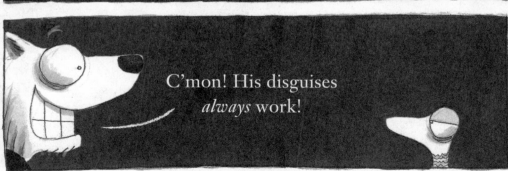

C'mon! His disguises *always* work!

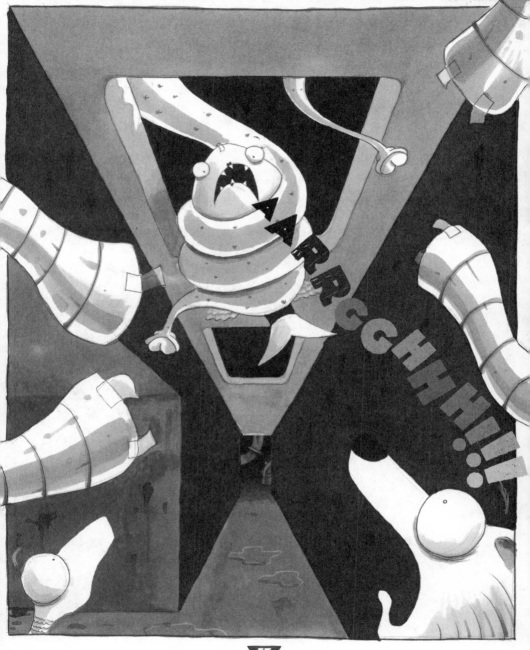

· CHAPTER 4 ·

AROUND IN CIRCLES

It's so dark.
Why is it so dark?
It seems to be
getting darker . . .
Don't you think it's
REALLY dark?

YES! GREAT OBSERVATION!
IT'S DARK! WHAT DO YOU WANT?
A *COOKIE*?
OBVIOUSLY, IT'S DARK.

Give me a break!
I'm **TERRIFIED**!
Everyone's gone. Even Shark!
But we can't give up! If we just
keep searching I **KNOW**
we'll find them. We're getting
CLOSE, I can feel it.

Oh really? We're getting *close*?
Then how do you explain **THIS** . . .

It **MEANS** we've been **WALKING AROUND IN CIRCLES**.

Listen to me, Wolf . . .

I'll admit it, **PART OF ME** really does want to be a hero. It's true. Part of me really, *really* does. But you know what I've learned from following you around on all these stupid missions? Do you know what I've learned from every ridiculous situation you've put us in?

DO YOU?

I've learned I'm *not* a hero.
I know you want me to be one . . .

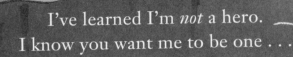

But I'm really, really not.

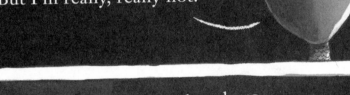

I know **YOU** want to be a hero.
And who knows—
MAYBE YOU ARE.
But I also think that you're **CRAZY**.
And I think, one day, you'll make
just one too many stupid decisions
and you **WILL** go and get
yourself eaten by an alien.
And, Wolf?

I think that day is today.

I've never had a friend before, Wolf. And even though I do call you an idiot kind of a lot . . . I know that you're the best friend I'll ever have. And I don't want to lose you. So . . .

Please get in the escape pod with me.

You know I can't, Mr. Snake.

And you know why, too.

I can't **MAKE** you do anything, buddy. What you do next is up to you. There's the **ESCAPE POD**. If you really want to leave, then go ahead, get in and go. But I have a feeling that you'll do the right—

WHAT?!
I didn't think you'd actually get in!

Why? Because of my little speech? Well, yeah, I meant it and everything, but there's an

ALIEN WITH BUTT HANDS
out there, so basically,

ALL BETS ARE OFF
and—

What?

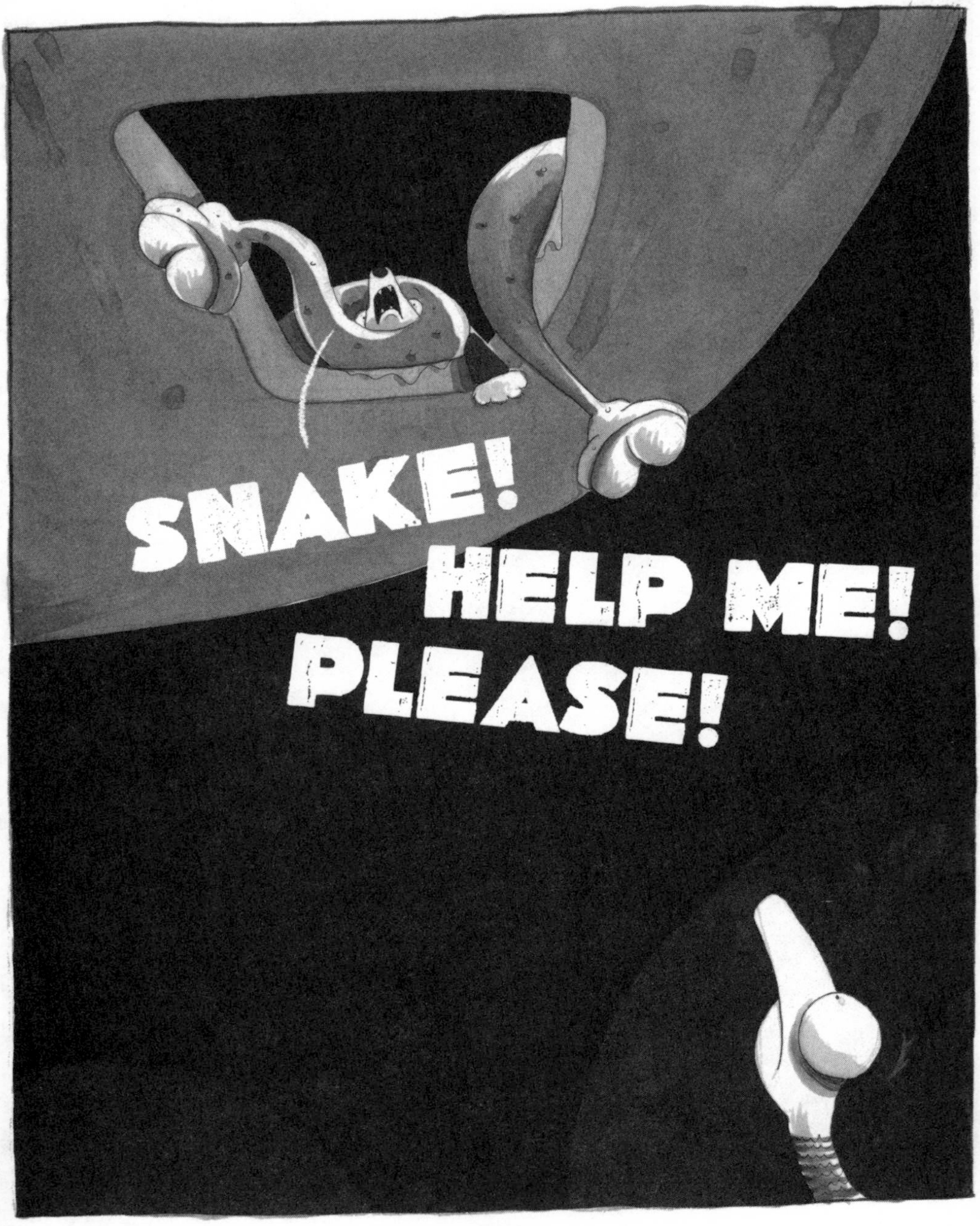
SNAKE!
HELP ME!
PLEASE!

· CHAPTER 5 ·
THE PIT OF DOOM

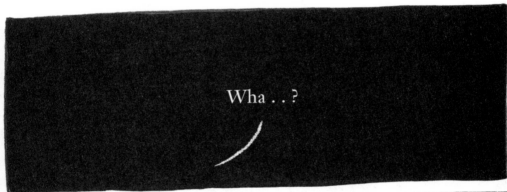

What **IS** this stuff?

I can't say for certain,
but I'm pretty sure it's
DRIED ALIEN SNOT,
hermano.

Piranha!

Hey, Wolfie. I've got to be honest—we were kind of hoping next time we saw you, you'd be **RESCUING US**.

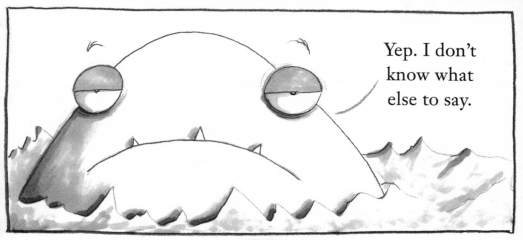

It's true. We're happy to see you, but I think we're all pretty disappointed, too.

Yep. I don't know what else to say.

Don't worry, guys! I think you're forgetting something . . .

Mr. Snake!

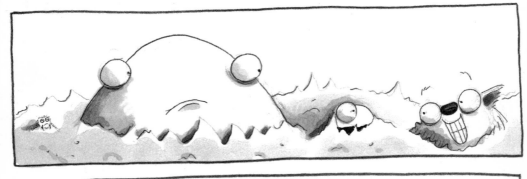

Is that meant to be funny?

No! I believe in him the way I believe in **ALL OF YOU!**

I'm kind of offended by that, *hermano*.

C'mon, guys! I bet he's coming up with a plan to save us **RIGHT NOW!**

LET ME SHOW YOU...

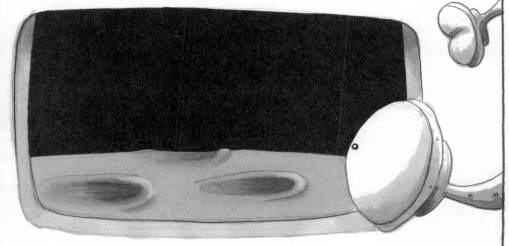

What a surprise.

Yeah. What a shocker.

I can't believe he left us . . .

REALLy?! You ACTUALLY CAN'T BELIEVE IT?!

· CHAPTER 6 ·
THE END OF THE ROAD

Hey, you! Butt hands! When you **FART**, is it from a single tentacle or do all the disgusting things go off at once?

WELL, I'M NOT SURE, LITTLE FISHY....

WELL, NO ONE TAKES MUCH NOTICE OF SILLY LITTLE GUINEA PIGS. SO I WAS ABLE TO STUDY YOUR PLANET VERY CAREFULLY WITHOUT ANYBODY NOTICING . . .

And what did you learn?

APART FROM THE FACT THAT PIRANHAS AND SHARKS DON'T NEED TO BE IN WATER AS MUCH AS YOU'D THINK?

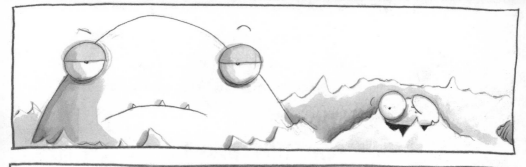

Yeah. Apart from that.

I LEARNED THAT YOUR PLANET IS HELPLESS.

AND IT WILL BE MINE.

I feel so stupid. I thought you were doing all of this just because you didn't like being **CUTE** and **CUDDLY**.

OH, THAT WASN'T A LIE. ON MY PLANET, I AM CUTE AND CUDDLY. AND I HATE IT. DON'T GET ME STARTED.

Is your name even Marmalade?

YOU COULDN'T PRONOUNCE MY REAL NAME, WOLF.

Try me.

My name is KDJFLOERHGCOINWERUHCG LEIRWFHEKLWJFHXALHW.

Yeah.
Well,
whatevs.

What do you want with us, KDJFLOERHGCOINWERUHCG LEIRWFHEKLWJFHXALHW?

WHAT DO I WANT WITH **YOU?** I WANT TO **EAT** YOU. BUT NOT BEFORE I SHOW YOU THE **DESTRUCTION** OF YOUR PLANET!

Yeah, yeah. That sounds great, KDJFdddd— whatever, and yeah, we all saw your weird, creepy **WEAPONS**, but you know what? You don't stand a chance!

OH REALLY? AND WHY'S THAT?

Because there's only **ONE** of you and you're no match for **AGENT FOX** and the **INTERNATIONAL LEAGUE OF HEROES!**

HMMM. THAT FOX IS VERY CLEVER...

BUT GUESS WHAT?

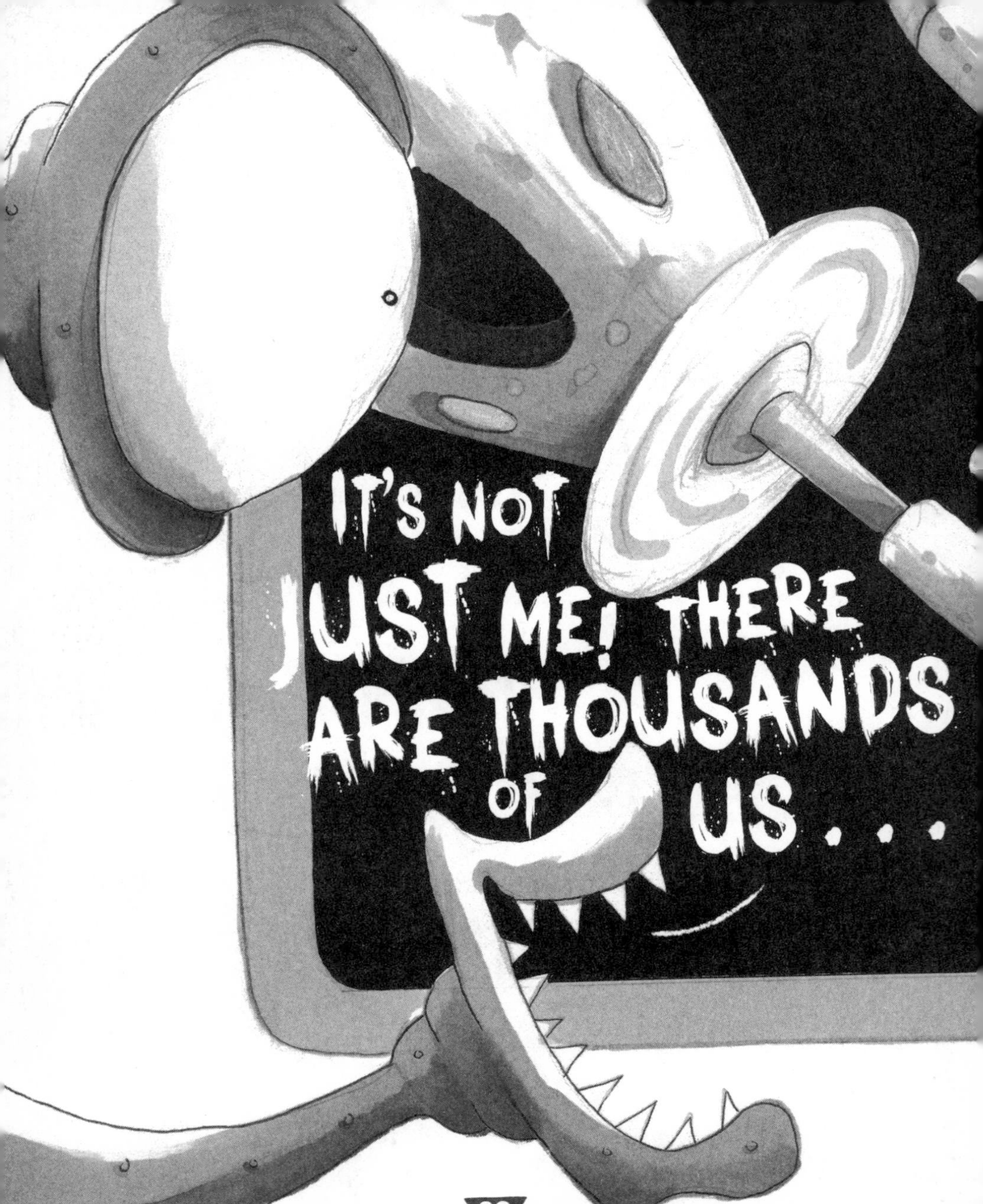
IT'S NOT JUST ME! THERE ARE THOUSANDS OF US . . .

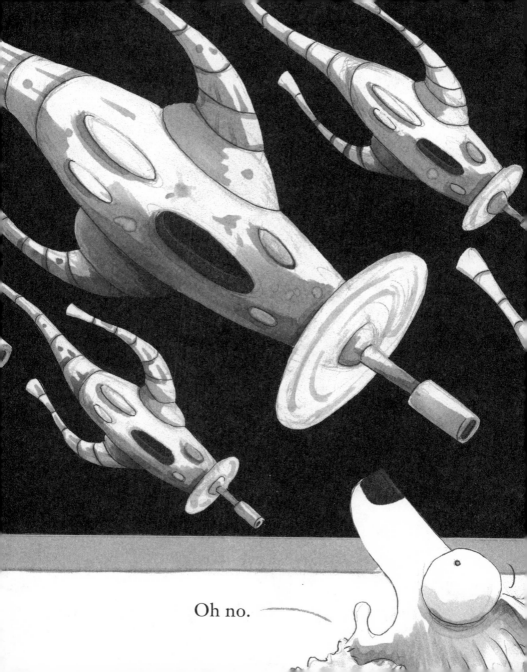

Oh no.

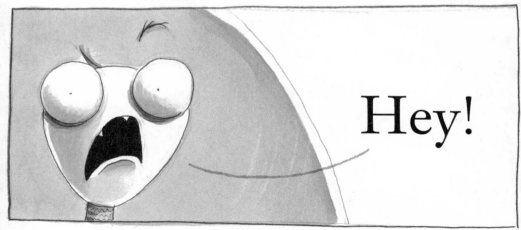

· CHAPTER 7 ·
PICK ON SOMEONE YOUR OWN SIZE

Bring it, guinea pig.

He's beating the alien
with his own butts!

EVERYONE, HOLD ON TO SOMETHING!

DANGER!
OUTER DOOR

CLUNK!

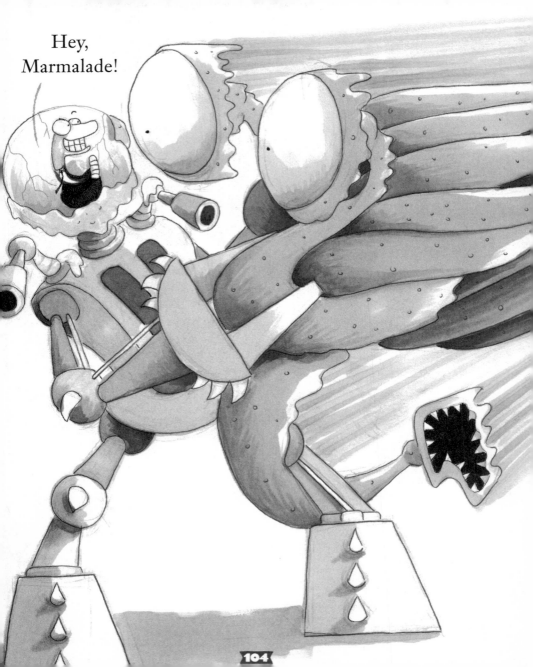

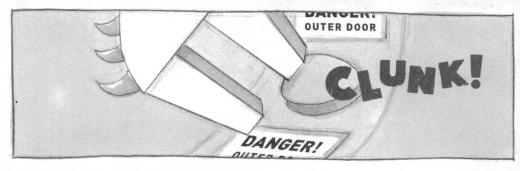

I guess I just finally got sick of being a Bad Guy.

Hey, *chicos*!

As much as I want to dance my dance of joy right now, there's a whole

ALIEN ARMY OUT THERE WAITING TO DESTROY EARTH!

We need to get home and warn **AGENT FOX.**

You're right. Let's get out of here, guys. But the good news is, this alien army doesn't have a **LEADER** anymore, thanks to YOU, Mr. Snake!

VOOMP!

AND MY FRIENDS LET ME BACK IN.

Wait a minute!

Did you just call him **KDJFLOER HGCOINWERU HCGLEIRWFHEK LWJFHXALHW?!**

GET THEM!

· CHAPTER 8 ·
THE POD

TO THE
ESCAPE POD!
HURRY!

I'm sorry, Legs, I had to fire off the first pod to **TRICK** Marmalade. How long will it take you to prep another one?

I'll do it as fast as I can, Mr. Hero!

Snake, I'm so proud of you! I mean . . . *how did you get that weapon thing to work?!*

I just . . . figured it out.

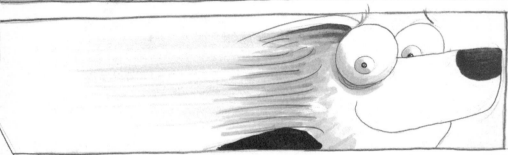

WHOOOA!
And there's goo all over the floor! **CAREFUL!**

S K I D !

I don't know what's worse—their crusty snot or their **SLIPPERY DROOL!**

That's it!
THE DROOL!
Everyone—GET ON
MY BACK!

Now hold on **TIGHT.**

Legs, I hate to rush you but—

I'm on it . . .

I don't mind rushing you!

HURRY, CHICO!

I'm on it!

Everyone, get in!

Um . . .

Um, *WHAT*?!

There's a setting here that kind of bothers me. I'm not sure what it means.

WHO CARES WHAT IT MEANS?!

JUST GET IN HERE AND SEND US BACK TO EARTH!

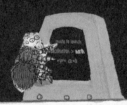

Yeah . . . OK . . .
I guess it'll be OK . . .

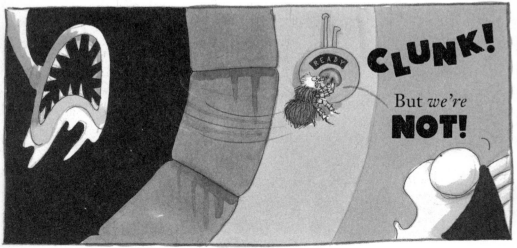

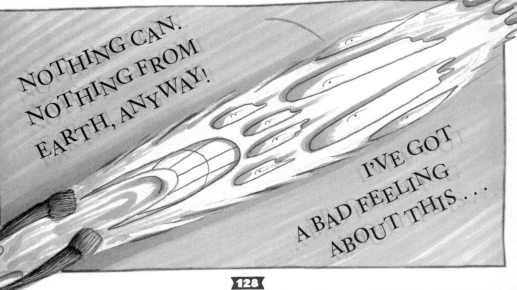

· CHAPTER 9 ·
OUT OF THE FRYING PAN, INTO THE—
HANG ON, THAT'S NOT INVENTED YET...

I can't lie, *chicos*. I thought there'd be a crowd waiting to welcome us. I've got my party pants on . . .

Yeah. And we have to warn Agent Fox.

Where is everyone?

Maybe we're just in the **WRONG SPOT.**

Did we land in another country or something?

Uhhhh, no. As far as I can tell, we've landed right back where we arranged to **MEET AGENT FOX.**

What do you mean, Legs? We're in the **MIDDLE OF NOWHERE**. You must be reading that thing wrong.

Hmmm. I wish I was . . .

Don't stress, guys! We're home! That's the main thing. We're home, but this time it's *different*. This time we're **HEROES!**

Ohhhhh. Being heroes isn't the only thing that's different . . .

What do you mean, Legs?

Well, remember that setting that was bothering me? It seems . . . it was the control for a slightly

DIFFERENT KIND OF TRAVEL . . .

You mean, that's the thing that made us go so **FAST?**

Well, maybe . . . but that's not what I mean . . .

Spit it out, Spider! **WHERE ARE WE?!**

Mr. Snake, the question isn't **"WHERE"** . . .

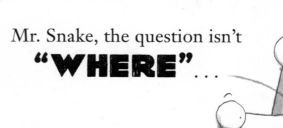

It's "**WHEN**."

Look!

Dudes . . . I think we **TIME-TRAVELED!**

year > 65,000,000 BC

location > earth

65 MILLION BC?! Are you kidding?! **65 MILLION BC?!** But that's when . . .

When, what?

Oh my stars! You're right! That's when there were . . .

That's when there were

WHAT?!

DINOS

TO BE CONTINUED . . .

IT'S ON.

Nothing can rival the **TERRIFYING** power of the **DINOSAURS**. Except maybe **THE BAD GUYS**! This is *all* **WRONG**. This is *all* **BAD**. This is *all* **AWESOME**!

Look for a super-sized adventure with
the **BAD GUYS** *in*
Do-You-Think-He-Saurus?!

With quizzes, games, and more bad-to-the-bone extras!